GIVEN AN OPPORTUNITY

LETTERS TO ARTHUR O. EVE

NEIL O'DONNELL

Author earnings from this book will be donated to an EOP fund at SUNY Buffalo State - The Jaelah Jenkins fund. This fund helps EOP students with college expenses.

Dear Mr. Eve,

I am just one of thousands of individuals who would likely not been able to get into college and pursue my dreams had it not been for the Arthur O. Eve Opportunity Programs. With the added support of EOP counselors and support staff, like my EOP counselor Dr. Roslyn Berkovitz, EOP students have overcome much and achieved personal and professional success through the programs you sponsored. Your devotion and dedication to helping others has touched so many individuals who in turn have reached out and helped countless children, women and men throughout the world. It is my hope that the letters contained within will help you see just how much of a better world you have made possible.

Sincerely,
Neil O'Donnell

A NOTE TO READERS

My parents taught me to thank everyone who helps you in life. This is my thank-you letter to Deputy Speaker Arthur O. Eve. The program he created and implemented provided me with an opportunity to attend college, an opportunity I am truly grateful for. I am also grateful for the conversations Mr. Eve and I had over the years. While our conversations were brief, he provided great personal and professional advisement that in turn helped me progress, excel, and succeed. For all Mr. Eve has done, I wanted to make certain that fellow students of the Arthur O. Eve programs would have easy access to information about the program's creator. In essence, I wanted to ensure that a record of Arthur O. Eve's achievements, sacrifices, and stewardship was available so incoming freshmen and EOP staff could learn about the man who continues to impact so many lives. For historians and those conducting political research, I hope this book provides references and insight that help guide your research efforts. I'm not a historian or a biographer. I'm an EOP graduate who wants to ensure Mr. Eve's work and accomplishments are forever remembered, especially by fellow opportunity program students Arthur O. Eve's legacy will help in the years to come. Take care.

ARTHUR O. EVE

Arthur Owen Eve, born on March 23, 1933, ultimately rose to political heights through which he successfully led efforts to aid individuals and communities, notably securing millions in aid for impoverished communities in Buffalo while setting precedent that likewise aided the poor throughout New York State and beyond. Known by many as "the conscience of the Legislature" (Thompson 2002, D5), Eve represented New York State and the Buffalo region in particular, serving as a senior member of the Ways and Means Committee and an influential member of the New York State Black and Puerto Rican Legislative Caucus. Throughout his time in politics, Eve continually took on political machines (Gilliam, 1975, p.284), taking on establishment groups and individuals to assure equality and justice for all.

After his birth in New York City, he soon moved to a housing project in Miami, Florida, with his mother and grandmother where he participated in sports and other recreational activities that were made readily available for area youth (Montgomery, 1992). His athleticism led to his achieving "All-

4

Florida" honors in basketball and his recognizing the importance of extracurricular activities to the successful development of youth. The lack of equivalent programming offered in Buffalo for children and adolescents ultimately served to help influence Arthur O. Eve's future run for political office. Today, Eve is remembered for his many awards which recently included his receiving a Liberty Award from the New York State Senate, the highest honor the body bestows upon an individual, as well as the 2016 Lifetime Achievement Award in Public Service from the Institute for Latino Studies. For those of us who are graduates of one of the Arthur O. Eve Educational Opportunity Programs, Dr. Eve is a hero.

Higher Education And Service

Arthur O. Eve was born in New York City in 1933 and lived there until his parents separated and he moved with his mother and grandmother to Miami, Florida (Institute for Latino Studies, 2016, Montgomery, 1992). After completing school, Eve attended West Virginia State College, but he was forced to withdraw due to a lack of funds (Kraus, 2005, p. 536; Williams et.al. 2005, p. 24). It was at this time he relocated to Buffalo, New York (1953) and soon entered the United States Army, where he served honorably from 1953 to 1955 (Mallegg, 2009, p. 383). Having arrived in Buffalo with less than $10 (Cornell, 2019), the military provided opportunity—an opportunity Eve used to the fullest. Rising to the rank of Corporal, Eve served overseas in Germany, where he found time to facilitate programming for orphans in addition to excelling in basketball and achieving All-Europe ranking (Levy and Miller, 1981, p. 54).

After serving, Eve returned to New York and continued his education at Erie Community College in Buffalo, where he attained an Associate's degree in 1957 (Williams et al, 2005, p. 24). Finding a job at the local Chevy plant, Eve's passion led him to seek a position working with youth, providing recreational and enrichment opportunities available in Florida yet not available in the Buffalo region. Directed to speak with a ward leader to see what openings were available, Eve was informed that such positions were given to "party loyals" (Levy and Miller, 1981, p. 55).

Building A Career

Frustrated with the political system hindering the development of programming for kids, Eve joined the Democratic party and was soon employed helping develop programs for youth. At the same time, Eve organized other community members, getting eligible residents to register to vote and inspiring individuals to get involved and understand what and how events, issues, and legislation were impacting their lives (p. 55). In time, Eve was elevated to a ward leader, a position that further directed him towards politics and battling established party hierarchies.

Assemblyman Eve

Eve first ran for office seeking a seat in the New York State Senate in 1965 (Williams et al, 2005, p. 24). Though unsuccessful in gaining the seat, Arthur O. Eve fought on and was elected in 1966 to the New York State Assembly, representing the 143rd district (and later representing the 141st district). His father, an immigrant from the Dominican Republic, Eve was the first Dominican American elected to serve in public office in the United States (Neuman, 2016, A20). It wasn't long before Eve would face entrenched political forces, and he never waivered during the trials he faced.

In one of many of his battles with New York Governor Nelson Rockefeller, Assemblyman Eve organized communities from throughout the Buffalo region to protest the barring by unions of Blacks from apprenticeships and, in turn, union membership. Telling the governor he would lie down in front of bulldozers if need be to prevent construction work from commencing in the spring (Levy and Miller, 1981, p. 57), Eve and his supporters effectively shut down construction projects in the region for nearly a whole year (1968-69) before the governor relented, paving the way for Blacks to achieve union membership and subsequent construction careers (p. 57). While Eve and his supporters did not obtain all the changes sought (Farrell, 1970, p. 45), a victory was still achieved, opening opportunities for minorities where previously there were none.

He would, in little time, rise to leadership positions, including both the Deputy Speaker of the Assembly and Deputy Majority Leader (Jeffries, 2000). With a constituency comprised of over 50% African Americans, Eve was instrumental in inspiring minority residents to vote and seek public office. Among his other achievements, reflecting his devotion to serving his constituents, Assemblyman Eve joined the New York State Black and Puerto Rican Legislative Caucus, only the second member of the caucus to represent an upstate district (Jeffries).

Eve also was a major contributor to and leader for efforts to organize African American communities to register to and actively vote (Levy and Miller, 1981, p. 65). From 1989 throughout the 1990s, the span of my undergraduate and graduate school years within the State University of New York system, I continually encountered Deputy Speak Eve as he gave moving speeches on and off campuses about the importance of voting by younger generations, particularly those from minority communities. Many of my fellow students and eventual EOP advisees were moved by Arthur O. Eve to register to vote after hearing him speak. What's more, many if not most of those who signed up, became active voters. Today, many of us alumni from Educational Opportunity Programs and Higher Education Opportunity Programs remain active voters, still emboldened by the words and wisdom of Arthur O. Eve. Many of us likewise remain voting advocates, encouraging others to register and actually show up on Election Day and vote. It is Deputy Speaker Eve who influenced many of us in this regard.

Both as Assemblyman for his Buffalo district and as Deputy Speaker of the New York State Assembly, Arthur O. Eve fought tirelessly to improve the lives of all New Yorkers, his style of action to keep pressuring the powers that be until they do what's right (Levy and Miller, 1981, p. 56). What programs and issues did he fight for?

- *Securing funding for K-12:* Ever concerned about youth, particularly academically and economically disadvantaged students, and calling what he perceived as the need for "drastic" educational reforms (Weiss, 1986), Arthur O. Eve routinely brought political friends and adversaries together to restore funding to K-12 programs periodically cut from governors' budgets. This includes leading efforts to protect "after-school tutorial, remedial and employment programs for inner city children" (Eve, 1995, p.12).
- *Securing contracts for businesses owned by women and minorities:* Arthur O. Eve never stopped in his efforts to level the playing field as he fought for funds and other supports for woman and minority-owned businesses (Kraus

2005:536). He was also instrumental in the successful fight to gain women and minorities access to jobs, even threatening to "lie down in front of bulldozers at state construction sites" until minorities were provided with equal access to apprenticeships and subsequent high-paying construction positions (Levy and Miller, 1981, p. 56).

- **Political knowledge and community insight:** In his capacity as a member of the NYS Assembly and the Black and Puerto Rican Caucus, Deputy Speaker Eve reached out to politicians to stress the need for interns to earn college credit while working for the Caucus (The Future of Black Studies, 1993, p. 536). The move would provide future leaders with greater insight to the concerns, needs, and obstacles faced by minority communities within New York State and beyond.

- **Tax amnesty:** With families struggling to make ends meet, the burden of financial penalties for late payment of taxes only acerbated the struggles of middle- and lower-income households. To counter this, Eve introduced legislation that would allow the waiving of "late penalties" for taxpayers, a program that some argued could generate well over $100 million, money that would then help balance the state budget (Long Island Business News, 2002).

- **Gaining access for disadvantaged students to higher education:** To this day, Arthur O. Eve continues fighting to assure disadvantaged students gain an equal opportunity to enter college. With SUNY's Educational

Opportunity Program, one of Eve's crowning achievements, it is only fitting that EOP and its sister program HEOP were ultimately renamed the Arthur O. Eve Educational Opportunity Programs for Education.

- **Work-release programs:** Eve stated that his attention to prisons and reforming the incarceration and treatment of convicted felons began in the late 1960s, when an elderly woman sought his assistance in getting transportation to Attica to see her son (Levy and Miller, 1981, p. 58). Driving the woman to Attica, Eve witnessed firsthand the injustices within the criminal justice system. As Eve's actions during the Attica Uprising would illustrate, he sought to establish guidelines and measures to ensure inmates received humane and just treatment. Beyond simply introducing legislation to reform the draconian prison conditions that he encountered at Attica, Eve sought to install measures that placed emphasis on the rehabilitation of inmates, which included his backing vocational training, work-release programs, and halfway houses to help parolees successfully transition back into communities (Schulman, 1993).

- **Informing the community:** Arthur O. Eve was recognized by even his political adversaries as someone who fought hard for his constituents, acting to get things done right rather than acting out of "animosity" (Montgomery, 1992). Ever the "conscience" of the Legislature, Eve also continually sought ways to inform his district and people throughout New York State on important issues of the day and related legislative or general political action, even holding regular Saturday radio broadcasts on WUFO (Gates and Fairbanks, 1989). To this day, Eve encourages everyone to take notice of the world and actions around them and stay informed in order to make the best choices in life and the voting booth.

- ***Serving the children:*** Arthur O. Eve focused much of his energy on helping improve the world and expanding the opportunities for children. From his early efforts to open recreational centers for youth in the 1960s to later in life, whether fighting for aid for literacy programs or organizing community members to discuss ways to help and engage children and adolescents in his district and statewide, making the world a better place for the young remains a primary objective of Eve, even to this day.

Through all his accomplishments, Arthur O. Eve consistently brought stakeholders together, helped identify the root cause of an issue, and facilitated negotiations to address the needs of New Yorkers. While no politician can be successful at every attempt, for me it is the attempts that matter a great deal. Successful more times than not, Arthur O. Eve always kept working to resolve issues and deliver needed resources and services to better the lives of fellow New Yorkers.

The Educational Opportunity Program

Vice President Al Gore recognized Arthur O. Eve as an "innovative thinker", particularly in areas of education and career training (Boyd, 1998). Given the Deputy Speaker's accomplishments in providing greater access to higher education while also securing more funding for K-12 schools statewide, it's hard to argue with the Vice President.

For K-12 schools, Arthur O. Eve fought tirelessly, negotiating deals with politicians throughout the state to make certain Buffalo received needed funding, which included helping to secure funds to end a lawsuit between the city of Buffalo and the teacher's union (Precious, 2000). Throughout his career, Eve helped the Buffalo metropolitan area acquire tens of millions of dollars more than it would have otherwise received. That calculates into millions more for student needs: teachers, classes, aides, nurses, food, books, and countless other supplies.

Beyond securing funds, Deputy Speaker Eve also fought rigorously to protect support programming (Eve, 1995). If the state made efforts to remove any educational supports within the Buffalo school system, Eve was there, rallying support from constituents, legislators, and anyone else who could assist. Today, School 61 in Buffalo bears the Deputy Speaker's name: The Arthur O. Eve School of Distinction. An appropriate honor given Eve's efforts, but Eve didn't stop at getting students through high school as he recognized the critical importance of continued education, whether pursuing a trade or a profession requiring college education. For economically disadvantaged students, higher education of any kind was often out of the question, not just for lack of funds to pay for college or a trade school program, but also for a lack of preparation in high school beforehand. The academic rigor of poorer school districts reduced as funds for necessary supports was oftentimes nonexistent; students faced difficult odds of higher education success. Enter Arthur O. Eve!

After witnessing the effectiveness of SEEK, a program developed by Percy Sutton, Arthur O. Eve led efforts that ultimately secured funds with which SUNY created the SEEK and Educational Opportunity Program in 1967 (Boyd, 1998). After successfully securing $500K in state funds, Arthur O. Eve created the SEEK/Educational Opportunity Program (EOP), with the first group of EOP students entering college at SUNY Buffalo State in 1967. While Eve collaborated with an array of stakeholders to better equip K-12 schools to, in turn, better prepare students for college, EOP provided funds and resources for high school graduates who lacked academic skill sets necessary for college success. EOP students to this day receive a variety of support beyond some funding. The bulk of the supports are in the form of academic resources and to this day, the EOP and Higher Education Opportunity Program (HEOP) departments throughout the state continue to offer these resources with great success.

Upon acceptance to an EOP or HEOP program, students generally attend an intensive summer program, usually between three and six weeks in length. These summer programs provide students with a taste of college coursework along with aides, including tutoring and peer mentoring. Likewise, EOP/HEOP counselors provide academic and career guidance while also connecting students with campus and/or community resources an individual student might need to tackle personal obstacles that may make college success difficult. During the academic year, EOP/HEOP students continue to receive access to tutoring and mentoring while also maintaining contact with their program counselor. These programs also offer additional supports, ranging from academic skills workshops, computer labs, career research aides, and access to lectures by guest speakers who cover a range of topics including health and wellness, career networking, studying abroad, and finding internships. Specific programming developed through EOP and HEOP programs includes:

- ***Tutoring resources:*** EOP and HEOP programs have long instituted professional and peer tutors to provide academic support to program students. Often ahead of the curve, EOP and HEOP tutors implemented rigorous training for their tutors, either employing certified master tutor trainers to teach tutors, or having tutors complete certified training through organizations such as the College Reading and Learning Association (CRLA).

- ***Summer programming for incoming freshmen:*** EOP and HEOP programs often require incoming freshmen to participate in three- to six-week summer programs where students complete college-level coursework (often earning three-six college credits) and attend workshops aimed at developing students' critical thinking and study skills. EOP and HEOP summer programs are geared towards helping students successfully transition from high school to college, and it is these summer initiatives that help in increasing the programs' retention and graduation of students.

- ***Summer enrichment programming and workshops.*** The long summer break that college students have provides a great chance for students to recharge and prepare for the next academic year. While this break helps restore students after the rigors of the previous academic year, students often struggle to get back into college success habits during the first couple weeks of the fall semester. During that transition period, students often struggle with assignments and class assessments. To counter this, EOP and HEOP programs have introduced summer programs and workshops, which provide students with ongoing opportunities to utilize their reading comprehension and critical-thinking skills. For students who participate, they often start the fall semester off strong and end up with a fall term GPA higher than other students (O'Donnell, 2012).

- *Freshman peer mentoring:* To continue the assistance initiated during EOP/HEOP summer programs, most opportunity programs connect freshmen with a peer mentor who helps in guiding the new freshmen through the rigors and many pitfalls encountered by most undergraduates. Whether it's a mentor sharing study strategies, coaching students in effectively utilizing campus academic resources, or showing new students where to get the best food on or off campus, these mentors contribute to the ongoing success of EOP and HEOP programs in their retaining and graduating students.

- *Sophomore success programming:* A more recent development within Arthur O. Eve Opportunity Programs focuses on providing continued guidance to sophomores to bolster the success of second-year students. As with SUNY Buffalo State's Sophomore Success Program, participating students are provided with peer mentoring and academic skills workshops aimed at helping students excel academically and personally. These programs have been shown to help students improve their GPA while enhancing their abilities in time management, test preparation, and stress management.

- ***Career coaching:*** Beyond academic supports, EOP and HEOP staff have provided career coaching since 1967. In addition to making higher education accessible to students, opportunity program counselors also prepare students for a successful transition between college life and career life. From connecting freshmen and sophomores to career centers and relevant faculties for guidance, to facilitating internships for juniors and seniors, opportunity program staff's career assistance has led to students finding a career path best suited to them and finding related employment after graduation. For EOP and HEOP counselors, it's a matter of keeping students focused on specific steps throughout every year of their undergraduate career.

- ***Financial guidance through college and beyond:*** The complexities of college financial aid are beyond frustrating. As many EOP and HEOP students are the first generation in their families to attend college, they oftentimes do not have family who can help them navigate federal and New Nork State grants and loans. Opportunity program staff provide the extra support needed to make certain students know due dates for submitting annual financial-aid forms and to assure students are connecting regularly with a college's financial-aid staff to better understand the financial-aid process and requirements. The assistance provided often includes annual workshops through which staff assist opportunity students with completing both the FAFSA and New York TAP applications. Beyond financial-aid concerns, opportunity program staff continually provide guidance to students on how to manage money, build savings, and navigate the minefields that are credit cards. These financial lessons are often taught directly by finance professionals from neighborhood banks, credit unions, and accounting firms.

- *Support groups for women and men:* EOP and HEOP programs take a holistic approach in supporting their students. Beyond getting students into college and being successful academically, counseling staff spend considerable time providing personal support as students face the rigors of college life. In time, the counseling component expanded to include support groups for women and men, the developing support systems especially impactful for minority students who often feel "isolated" and "left out" at the colleges and universities they intend. These groups offer a comfortable atmosphere for sharing ideas, experiences and stresses, the counselor-led groups providing support as needed. Opportunity program support groups often become active in campus-wide efforts at community service to the college and the neighboring communities. Since 1989, whenever I have interacted with Arthur O. Eve, I have always seen him lending an ear and guidance to students while also encouraging students to take what they've learned and share it with others. It is in these support groups that I see Arthur O. Eve's teachings most. Whether as Deputy Speaker Eve, Dr. Eve, Assemblyman Eve, or Mr. Eve, he always inspires others to care about and share with others.

- ***Textbook libraries and loan programs.***
Textbooks, a critical tool in most college courses,
cost an exorbitant amount of money, money
students often don't have. Consequently, many
students attempt to tackle their classes without a
textbook, which makes it hard for the students to
learn course material and comprehend lectures. To
combat the textbook dilemma, multiple EOP and
HEOP programs purchase textbooks and then loan
them to students either through reserve collections
at the college libraries or directly through the EOP
or HEOP office. Now equipped with textbooks,
students have a greater chance to excel in their
respective classes.
- ***Study skills workshops.*** Most students enter
college lacking study skills needed to attain a
comprehensive understanding of course material
and, in turn, achieve academic success. EOP and
HEOP programs often provide workshops
throughout every semester where academic
advisors and tutors train students in effective study
skills, which includes reading comprehension,
research strategies, essay development, test
preparation, and stress management, the latter
often an obstacle throughout all stages of a
student's academic career. In connection with
these workshops, EOP and HEOP programs often
produce study skills guides/pamphlets to distribute
to students to help students better retain the
information presented in workshops, and to reach
students unable to attend study skill workshops due
to classes and other commitments.

- ***Technology loan programs and computer labs.*** College students rely on a mix of technologies every semester, from computers to graphic calculators. Given the importance of such technology to student success, multiple opportunity programs invest in laptop computers, calculators, tablets, and other tech, which they then loan to students for a set amount of time. Opportunity programs also often acquire desktop computers, which are set up in a lab on campus, providing students with access to computers and printers so that they can complete research papers, essays, and other assignments. Computer labs are generally staffed with computer/technology tutors and technicians to help students learn to utilize both computer hardware and programming.

- ***Organized study halls.*** Finding a quiet space on a college campus in which to study, prepare for exams, and complete research papers is not always an easy task. To address this reality, EOP and HEOP programs throughout New York State have created and maintain rooms in which students can be assured of a quiet workspace, a space often equipped with computers, tutors, and peer mentors. These spaces often become a home away from home for students, providing academic and personal support in an environment designed to help students excel.

- ***GRE, GMAT, MCAT & LSAT preparation workshops.*** For students pursuing a graduate degree, the Graduate Record Exam (GRE) and similar standardized tests are a hurdle prospective graduate students need to confront, a part of the admissions process similar to the SAT and its use in determining undergraduate admissions. Like the SAT, these examinations are comprehensive, exhaustive, and difficult assessments to manage, particularly when an undergraduate student is also still completing coursework for their Bachelor's degree. While many private businesses offer prep classes to help students prepare for these exams, cost of attendance can range from several hundred dollars to well over $2000, an amount well out of reach for many opportunity programs' students. In answer to the need for helping students prep for these assessments, EOP and HEOP programs often run annual workshops through which trained instructors provide comprehensive tutoring and coaching, a resource that has proven to help students attain scores that in turn open the door to graduate school.

Now known as the Arthur O. Eve Opportunity Programs, EOP and HEOP programs have helped thousands of New Yorkers graduate and find career success as teachers, entrepreneurs, doctors, accountants, psychologists, attorneys, judges, police officers, social workers, politicians, historians, nurses, counselors, business executives, architects, and accomplished scientists in fields ranging from Anthropology to Zoology. The effectiveness of the Arthur O. Eve Opportunity Programs reaches beyond just its students. EOP and HEOP initiatives statewide have led to the development of similar academic and mentoring programming through other campus departments worldwide, with opportunity program staff presenting on their initiatives. Today, EOP and HEOP programming serve as models for the creation of supports that lead to greater student success and retention across the board. In many ways, Arthur O. Eve's vision and efforts ultimately provided academic and career guidance for all New York students.

Calming The Storm

The assassination of Dr. Martin Luther King, Jr. set Buffalo on the brink of chaos, as it did in communities throughout the United States. In the immediate time after Dr. King's death, Arthur O. Eve and other local politicians reached out to Buffalo communities, successfully quelling violence. From locking arms with fellow politicians and Buffalo citizens in Lafayette Square to visiting area schools with Councilman Charles Volkert and police officer Ted Kirkland (Cichon, 2016; Taylor, 1998, p. 109), Assemblyman Eve helped pull Buffalo through tumultuous events that may have otherwise torn Buffalo's communities further apart than they already were.

Attica

Assemblyman Eve's work-release programs, which he championed later in his political career, were built upon his long-standing fight for rights and equality for incarcerated citizens. In particular, Arthur O. Eve and other progressive leaders fought to bring light to the glaring reality that African Americans, Latinos, and other minorities were disproportionately imprisoned when compared to white convicts, a lack of funding for bail and expert legal representation significant hardships to overcome. The lack of economic and educational opportunities for minorities throughout America was a direct cause for this reality. While civil rights legislation passed during the 1960s aimed to curb discrimination minorities faced, the reality was that discrimination throughout the country remained an overwhelming hurdle, particularly for those who did not speak English.

Once incarcerated, minorities faced additional barriers as whites, Less than 40% of Attica's prisoner population in the early 1970s held the vast majority of higher paying jobs available to convicts within the prison (Thompson, 2016, p. 12). As inmates were provided with limited resources each month, including only one bar of soap and one roll of toilet paper (p. 8), the earnings from prison work could have made a significant difference for inmates—at least if they could have attained one of the higher paying job opportunities and thereby afford daily essentials in the commissary.

Prior to the 1971 uprising at Attica Prison, New York State had already experienced upheavals in state penitentiaries in the NYC region and across upstate; one of the most impactful was the fall 1970 revolt at Auburn Correctional Facility, where inmates took correction officers and other support personnel hostage in response to overcrowding and poor living conditions. In response to the standoff, the involved prisoners secured an opportunity to present their grievances and demands to a prison official and an assurance that those involved in the revolt would face no punitive action or abuse (p. 24). Once the hostages were freed, the inmates' demands were heard, but punishments in the form of beatings, isolation, and criminal charges were doled out (p. 24).

In the aftermath of the Auburn revolt, Assemblyman Arthur O. Eve visited the Auburn Correctional Facility to assess the living conditions of inmates, as well as to check on those inmates held most responsible for the revolt. His discoveries during his visit horrified many. What is known is that after his 1970 visit to Auburn Correctional Facility, Assemblyman Eve warned of the "inhumane" treatment of prisoners (Thompson, 2016, p. 25).

On September 8, 1971, tensions began to build because of a scuffle between two inmates. Correction officers, including Lieutenants Richard Maroney and Robert Curtis, confronted the involved inmates, one of whom was Leroy Dewer, a participant of the 1970 uprising at Auburn who had been sent to Attica (Wicker, 2011, p. 10). By day's end, Dewer and inmate Ray Lamorie were taken from their cells to solitary confinement, actions that severely angered inmates (p. 14). To complicate matters, many prisoners feared both inmates involved had been severely beaten (Thompson, 2016, p. 49). In the morning, on September 9, 1971, the inmates' collective anger over the previous day's incidents, the harsh living conditions, and the lack of response to inmate grievances presented in recent months to prison officials, led to a group of prisoners attacking Attica's corrections officers and taking control of multiple areas of the prison. During the conflict, multiple officers were severely beaten while others were spared from intense retaliation, inmates often protecting those officers and civilian employees who were deemed "good guys" and respectful of prisoners (NYS Special Commission, 1972, p. 176; Thompson, 2016, pp. 56-57; Wicker, 2011, p. 16).

Upon hearing of the uprising, Assemblyman Eve quickly made his way to the prison. It was not long before Eve was apprised of the situation, and the assemblyman ultimately became one of the first individuals, along with Herman Schwartz, to enter "D Yard" where prisoners had gathered and where Eve and Schwartz received the inmates' demands (NYS Special Commission, 1972, p. 206; Thompson, 2016, pp. 75-76). Known for his work on behalf of incarcerated citizens, Eve immediately proved a calming force in the turmoil, his presence helping to soothe tensions evident at the first meeting between inmates and Eve (Thompson, 2016, p.74). Early on in negotiations, Eve arranged to have a group of inmates from D Yard to inspect other areas of the prison now under control of prison authorities. Inmates in D Yard worried other inmates, particularly those in custody in C Block, were being physically punished in retaliation for what had transpired, as occurred to participants after the Auburn uprising (p. 78). After assurances from multiple observers did not alleviate such concerns, Eve helped arrange for a small group of inmates to tour C Block (NYS Special Commission, 1972, p. 224; Thompson, 2016, pp. 84-85).

Arthur O. Eve ultimately assumed a leadership role for the observers who tried to peacefully end the standoff between the inmates and New York correctional and executive authorities. Amnesty for the inmates was one of the demands sought by those who participated in the uprising; it was likewise something that Eve and other observers, knowing the precarious situation faced by all, had argued for as well (NYS Special Commission, 1972, pp. 270-271; Wicker, 2011, p. 257). For Eve and other observers, the presence of New York Governor Rockefeller was critical so that the state's chief executive could better evaluate and understand the tension and the collective anger and frustration the assembled state officers were harboring, and the likely extent of extreme violence (NYS Special Commission, 1972, p. 271). However, the governor did not go to Attica.

Complicating things further, a message was sent to the inmates by Russell Oswald, the Commissioner of Correctional Services, which requested that the state personnel being held hostage be released and that inmates accept terms presented by Eve and the other observers. The observers, including Eve, believed this action shattered the trust they had developed with the inmates, because the observers were actually just relaying what they considered the "best deal" the inmates would receive from the commissioner (p. 278). The prospect of reentering the yard for further negotiations became a dangerous proposition at that point as the inmates would likely have seen the statement as the observers agreeing to terms without consent of the inmates (Thompson, 2016, p. 145). Eve, however, worked to get back to the inmates to salvage the situation. Before being allowed into D Yard, however, the governor required any observers entering the prison to sign waivers protecting the state from lawsuits in the event an observer was injured or killed (p. 147).

Faced with such a grim choice, Eve and several other observers still entered Attica Prison to meet with inmates once again.

While reading Heather Ann Thompson's Pulitzer Prize-winning account of Attica, *Blood in the Water* (2016), I was overwhelmed by Thompson's recounting of a statement by Richard Clark, one of the inmates leading the others. Upon Eve and the other observers entering D Yard and returning to the negotiating table set up by the inmates, the commissioner's words still fresh in their minds, Clark informed them that some of the inmates would love to kill them (p. 147). The observers were able to convince the inmates that they were not aware of the message the commissioner planned to send. Fortunately, the inmates again recognized Eve and company's genuine wish to aid the prisoners and assure a peaceful solution.

Newsman/cameramen were allowed to speak with hostages, who reiterated the importance of the governor coming to Attica and that amnesty be granted. Yet the governor never came. After the uprising was ended with an assault by state forces, and interviews were conducted of survivors, inmates stated that the governor's presence would have likely led to a settlement (NYS Special Commission, 1972, p. 294).

On September 13, 1971, state authorities stormed Attica and regained control, their assault leading to the death of ten hostages and twenty-nine prisoners, with many others receiving critical wounds. In the aftermath, Assemblyman Arthur O. Eve joined other observers in touring the prison grounds, whereupon they witnessed the torture of inmates (Thompson, 2016, p. 211), with beatings being observed by prison staff days after the retaking of Attica (p. 216), and the targeting of minorities by prison personnel even observed by national guardsmen brought in to assist with restoring order (pp. 211-212). Rumored atrocities on the part of inmates likely contributed to the severity of the treatment they received during and after authorities reclaimed the prison, yet the rumors did not match facts found during autopsies; the hostages were all shot (Wicker, 2011, pp. 302-303). Observations were made by Assemblyman Eve regarding inmate L. D. Barkley, an inmate who was amongst those contributing to negotiations. Barkley was found dead from gunshot wounds to the back and chest after the state's assault, but Eve recalled seeing Barkley alive after prison personnel had assumed full control of Attica (NY State Special Commission, 1972, p. 396). What happened after the guards had regained control? The collective findings by witness observations, autopsies, and eventual investigations still leave many questions unanswered, though a judge ultimately ruled that authorities used excessive force in the retaking of the prison (Thompson, 2016, p. 460).

Eve would help spearhead prison reforms throughout his career (Levy and Miller, 1981, pp. 58-59). As for Governor Rockefeller, Assemblyman Eve led efforts to impeach the governor for using such lethal force at Attica "when a peaceful solution was clearly visible" (Gilliam, 1975, pp. 139-140). After Rockefeller's nomination for Vice President by President Gerald Ford in 1974, during Rockefeller's senate hearings, Assemblyman Eve testified, relaying the governor's decisions and actions regarding the Attica uprising. While the senate ultimately approved Rockefeller's nomination for the vice presidency, Arthur O. Eve clarified for many Americans what had transpired in Attica during September of 1971.

The Run For Mayor

In 1977, Assemblyman Eve made history once again by becoming the "first black Democratic mayoral candidate in New York State" history. Before a primary was held, many within the region's Democratic Party thought Eve would be a serious contender for the Democratic nomination (Carton, 1980).

An independent powerhouse within the Democratic Party, and the current Deputy Democratic Majority Leader of the New York State Assembly, Eve focused much of his campaigning on Buffalo's inner city. The primary results proved Eve was indeed a strong candidate, ending with well over 50% of eligible voters casting ballots, and 98% of the Democratic Party votes cast for Arthur O. Eve (Ena, 1990, p.27). Later that fall, when all votes were tallied in November for the general mayoral election, Assemblyman Eve ultimately lost to Conservative Party candidate, Jimmy Griffin (Borrelli et al, 1989). While apparent efforts within the region's Democratic Party may have helped Griffin in winning the general election (Levy and Miller, 1981, p. 54), over 75% of Buffalo's Black voters went to the polls, then ranking as one of the top three Black voter turnouts in American history (p. 53). Arthur O. Eve has long focused on getting eligible voters registered and then encouraging everyone to follow through, researching candidates and showing up on election day to cast a ballot. I have no doubt this energy and enthusiasm aided his election success. While not winning the mayoral election, Eve and his supporters showed the power held by the electorate in challenging and overcoming political party establishments.

For The Community

Eve's political career and community accomplishments are far-reaching—before, during, and after his years in the New York Assembly. Between leading efforts to generate HIV and AIDS awareness among Africa-American communities to serving as a leading voice for groups opposed to casinos, Eve was continuously at the forefront of efforts to protect communities in Western New York and statewide from harmful organizations, health and wellness threats, and legislation that threatened services for poor and minority communities.

In the mid-1990s, when many state-funded academic supports faced elimination, Deputy Speaker Eve reached out to representatives and residents of New York alike in a fight to preserve tutoring, job and college preparatory programs, which were vital to aiding children in preparing for life after school, particularly inner-city youth (Eve, 1995, p. 12). Even the Educational Opportunity Program and its sister programs were on the verge of elimination in the 1990s, programs that had produced graduates who went on to become successful teachers, medical doctors, nurses, engineers, psychologists, social workers, therapists, attorneys, judges, authors, and military personnel. Eve's leadership and efforts helped preserve many of the programs slated for cancelation, allowing thousands of New York students in K-12 and higher ed to continue to have access to those support resources they needed to complete their studies and prepare for career success. His efforts didn't end there. Within a short span of time, Eve rallied communities to make sure citizens registered to vote and had the means to go to voting centers when disabilities barred travel. Many of us who were college students in the SUNY system at this time were inspired by Eve and in turn encouraged our family and friends to register and vote. Additionally, we wrote legislators and called government offices to voice our concerns that such valuable programming was about to be canceled.

Eve wanted community members to be informed and serve as active participants in America's and New York's development. From his example and encouragement, thousands registered to vote. While it would be hard to measure Eve's impact on actual voter turnout, I know of a great number of college students who went to the polls after being inspired by Eve to take responsibility for the future development of our communities and the wellbeing of our family, friends, and neighbors.

Life After Public Office

In 2002, Arthur O. Eve, the Deputy Speaker of the New York State Assembly and representative of the 141st NYS district, retired from public office. However, rest and relaxation were far from his mind at the time. Deep-held concerns about struggling New York communities moved Eve to leave public office so he could "organize communities of color and to join with religious leaders to pressure the system", his hope that such efforts would resolve the lack of opportunity available for these communities (Hicks, 2002, B4).

Ever the advocate, Arthur O. Eve spoke with students throughout the state, those in K-12 as well as college students. He encouraged them to be active participants in the state and federal government, voting and making certain their voices were heard through letter-writing campaigns, marches, and getting on the phone to contact local representatives. Eve also met continuously with politicians, community leaders, and educators at all levels to continue the fight to preserve resources for education, healthcare, and employment. He was a regular attendee at EOP and HEOP events across the state, sharing his enthusiasm and wisdom with students, staff, and faculty, and to this day he never hesitates to take time to console, encourage or advise individuals facing enormous personal, academic or career hurdles.

In time, Eve created the Freedom, Justice and Hope Foundation, an organization that strove to provide educational assistance to urban youth, families, and "underperforming" schools through the development of education kits, advocacy for increased education funding with which to develop tutoring and mentoring services, and the facilitation of education workshops (Kraus, 2005, p. 536; Watson, 2005; Precious, 2003, B1). Collaborating with public institutions, local churches, and local politicians, Eve and his team successfully delivered educational resources while inspiring parents and children to take an active role in their own education and personal development. His work didn't stop there.

Ever the public servant, Eve continued to gather people and community members together to fight for needed resources for those most in need. His efforts continue to this day and inspire members of all generations to take a stand and speak up for justice, peace, and opportunity.

Legacy

It has been stated that Arthur O. Eve has done more to bring educational and financial opportunity to minority communities and the "economically disadvantaged" than any other state-level legislator throughout the country (Institute for Latino Studies, 2016). That is something I wholeheartedly concur with. From a statistics standpoint, the opportunity programs alone afforded thousands of high-school graduates the chance to be the first in their families to attend college. That opportunity opened more doors for individuals and their families, providing the means to escape poverty, achieve career success, and contribute to local communities throughout New York.

I remember during the mid-1990s, when Governor Pataki presented a budget that essentially eradicated most of the opportunity programs he and other legislators had enacted. Eve himself referred to it as "the budget of no hope" (Eve, 1995). Deputy Speaker Eve reached out to college students, EOP and HEOP graduates, and all of New York, and presented a case for the importance of the soon to be cut programs and the proposed tax cuts serving as the root cause of their demise. In that dark hour, Arthur O. Eve inspired many of us to look beyond ourselves and see that oppression of one of us meant the oppression of all of us. Advocacy efforts were ultimately successful in protecting the educational programs that had helped so many, who in turn helped communities throughout New York State through career success and public service. All said, since any biography would fall short of truly measuring Mr. Eve's impact on the world, let the following letters provide readers with insight into Arthur O. Eve's Legacy, a legacy he continues to build on each day as he emboldens men, women, and children to fight for justice and pursue their dreams.

LETTERS TO THE HONORABLE
ARTHUR O. EVE

Contained herein are letters written for Arthur O. Eve by EOP/HEOP students. The archive, now set up, will continue to collect letters while also ensuring Mr. Eve receives the letters. To those who submitted letters, thank you for contributing to this effort.

DEAR DEPUTY SPEAKER ARTHUR O. EVE:

We, the students of the Arthur O. Eve Educational Opportunity Programs, are forever thankful for your efforts to establish the educational and personal supports that aided our journeys through college and into our professional lives. We also continue to be inspired by your deeds of charity and public service, your words and actions driving each of us forward every day.

The following letters are from students of your opportunity programs, each individual sharing insights into their experiences while also expressing gratitude for you and for how the opportunity programs aided their overcoming obstacles and achieving success.

To the Honorable Arthur O. Eve,

My name is Carmen Villanueva-Horlacher and I am a SUNY Plattsburgh EOP graduate of the class of 1988. Dr. Arthur O. Eve, your innovative thinking in formulating the EOP most certainly had a profound effect on my life. I studied and graduated with a BS in Food and Nutrition.

I never knew and thought that I could go away for college. I am of Hispanic heritage and the first generation to attend college in my family. There existed a cultural barrier in my immediate family. By this I mean that no one went to college let alone go away to college. It was assumed that especially of the daughters to live nearby. I remember like it was yesterday an EOP counselor called my home on the day I had to leave for the summer pre-prep program and wanted to speak with my mother. My counselor wanted to let my mother know about the wonderful opportunity that was being offered to her daughter and that she should not forgo the chance. Of course, my mother was upset and crying mostly because she did not want to let me go. After that phone call, my mom said that I must go. So, there in the summer of 1984 my journey began.

The EOP of SUNY Plattsburgh was instrumental with my adjustment to college life. The program provided us with the money to take the greyhound bus to Plattsburgh. Along with providing books and a calculator for me to use. We even for a 6-week period were issued a $15 dollar stipend weekly for any personal incidentals we might need. The program taught us techniques on how to study as well as time and stress management skills in order for us to succeed. The staff was always there for us when we needed to talk. The program provided me not only the academic support but emotional support as well ... something that I needed. I had many personal hurdles and challenges to overcome since I was the first generation to go to college.

My sister Maribel Villanueva was going to pass up the opportunity to go college because she was embarrassed to apply for financial aid. Somehow, I managed to get her to apply for admission to college. Till this day, she thanks me for setting a good example for her to emulate. She too graduated from SUNY Plattsburgh EOP in 1996. Maribel now is the Director of Discipline for the Atlanta school system. I also have the passion to pass on to my daughters 10 and 14 years old now the importance of an education. My husband and I take the girls to college campuses locally in CNY and as well as Plattsburgh homecoming events throughout the years. I tell them that through education I was able to break the poverty cycle.

There were many moments in which EOP helped me during my undergraduate education. I remember getting a letter in my dorm mailbox that the director wanted to see me, and the letter had not indicated what was the reason for this meeting. Of course, I panicked and immediately thought I was in trouble for something. At the time, the Director was Keith Smith. Anyway, to make a long story short, he had a list in front of him and said that my midterm grades in organic chemistry was an A, and he advised me to possibly pursue a career in chemistry or the sciences. I gave a sigh of relief. The EOP staff where always keeping an eye on us and making sure that we knew our strong points. This is why I chose to pursue nutrition because the curriculum offered several courses in chemistry and science.

The EOP experience has taught me to be passionate with what I do because the future depends on it. The program taught me to be confident and persistent with regards to achieving my career goals. This program has served as a catalyst for me to have had a successful career as a WIC Nutritionist/Breastfeeding Coordinator. Currently, I volunteer my clinical expertise in lactation/breastfeeding within my community in Upstate New York. I have been helping mothers and the infant dyad through complicated medical challenges for 20 years. I do this at no charge, as I do not want financial difficulties to hinder someone who needs lactation care.

As I sum up this letter, I have tears of joy that I have come full circle as an individual because of EOP. Thank you Dr. Arthur O. Eve.

Carmen Villanueva-Horlacher
SUNY Plattsburgh

To the Honorable Author O. Eve,

In 2002, I was a participant in the Summer Training and Employment Program (S.T.E.P.) as a student from Kensington High School, which was the lowest performing high school in the City of Buffalo at the time. As most young students, my goal was to show up and get money the easiest way possible. During that year of service, I provided office support for what seemed to be a very busy man who would consistently run errands and work with his staff; kind of something that I had inspired to. Eventually, in the summer of 2005, I was blessed to be accepted into Canisius College's Higher Education Opportunity Program (HEOP), majoring in Criminal Justice and Sociology. My aspirations were to become a counselor, followed by becoming the CEO of a nonprofit organization that would serve individuals impacted by incarceration.

During my HEOP experience, there were many stigmas associated with HEOP and other related summer bridge program participants like me. However, HEOP prepared me for the rigor of Canisius' academics, also while leveraging my ability to successfully navigate through negative stereotypes and experiences that many of my peers encountered. The HEOP program also expedited my ability to understand my worth and value as an equally merited student. My assigned HEOP counselors guided my ambiguity, shifted my mindset and drove high standards, motivation and desire for success. The ongoing love and support from the program made retention easy. For HEOP's investment in my education, I felt that becoming a HEOP alumni was not an option.

There were three memorable moments and valuable leadership lessons that I absorbed while in HEOP. The HEOP summer program was my first memorable moment and initia-

tion. During that time, I was able to fully understand my investment and HEOP's investment in my future. I learned the value
of building a supportive team of people who had the same
mission, goals and value in education. With that, I learned that
the need for people engagement and collaboration was a neces-
sity for success.

The next leadership lesson was the importance of maintaining relationships with counselors during the school year.
Having a dedicated support system available provided me an
extra push forward. Additionally, the program provided a safe
space to vent about my two abstract experiences: the campus
life and my home life, which was much different from campus.
The supportive conversations made me feel safe physically,
psychologically and academically.

Lastly, graduation was the most impactful leadership
lesson. This lesson was bittersweet, as at this point I'd successfully achieved what many thought was impossible. I'd gone
from attending the lowest performing school to receiving a dual
degree at one of the best colleges in the Upstate New York area.
I left feeling assured to me that the sky could be the limit
despite walking across stage as the only student who graduated
from my group of peers who I built relationships with in the
program. This experience taught me a few things. The first
lesson taught me that no matter what, focus on my purpose and
mission is imperative to succeed. Even though relationships
were built, and bonds occurred, life can take people in many
directions. The other lesson that graduation taught me was that
receiving an education is a competitive, rigorous and humbling
process. Thus, it allowed me to test my dedication, commit-
ment and my limits. HEOP provided an opportunity to trust its
process and reduce my fear of failing. In 2009, as I waited to
receive my diploma, I came to realize that the man who I
worked for, who worked so diligently with his staff was you,

Mr. Author O. Eve. Hence, my overall lesson from being in HEOP. I learned that I would never take anything for granted and I would take advantage of every opportunity, whether the benefit or reason is fully understood as even a stranger can impact my life.

As a result, I have taken advantage of every opportunity for development, access and service. I have successfully applied the same knowledge, skills and abilities gained from the HEOP program during the rest of my academic and professional journey. I had the opportunity and privilege to receive a Master of Public Administration and currently in the final stages of completing a Doctor of Education in Executive Leadership. Professionally, I was able to become a human service and criminal justice counselor to now being an organizational leader, consultant and community impact professional. Without my start in HEOP, I am not sure where my life would be.

Going forward, it is crucial to support not only the next generation of students entering EOP and HEOP. It is also important to support my former HEOP peers who did not graduate after entering the program and those who are still figuring things out. Mr. Eve, you once said in an interview, "education is the number one civil rights issue of today, tomorrow and forever because our people have to compete with the world"...Because of the HEOP program, now I can. Going forward, I will vow to be available, encouraging to those in need and of continuous support of every phase in a prospective scholar's journey, just as you all were for me.

Cord Stone, MPA
Canisius College

Dear Arthur,

My name is Tanjin, and I an Engineer that travels the country to audit suppliers for my company that works with NASA and helps launch missions to send people to the moon and space. I am in the space program at my job and when I was a little girl, I was always so curious about Space. I would not be able to fulfill my dream without the EOP program. This program has helped me be the best version of myself. The EOP program at Buffalo State helped me adjust to college because it helped me understand time management and how to focus on my goals. I learned how to become much more disciplined with what I do with my free time. I ended up being on the Dean's list my first two semesters of College because the EOP program had always encouraged students to go for tutoring with any course that they are struggling with.

My counselor, Jude Jayatilleke, was amazing, and he always made me challenge myself even though sometimes I would be so stubborn. He was always there for my older sister and me. When I first came into college, I was young and naïve. I did not know what to do in life, but Mr.Jude always pointed me in the right direction.

The most memorable moment where EOP helped was providing a stipend for my books. I had some courses where I was not able to afford some of the books, but because of EOP, I was able to get the necessary tools I needed to become successful in College. I would not be a Senior Quality Engineer today without the help of EOP because of all the support I have gotten from my mentors and staff. I learned to always try to overcome every challenge I face in life.

Some of the lessons I learned to pass onto some younger generations is to always be relentless with any adversity you are facing. I remember the first few semesters of College were tough, but I became a better person to help others in need. I was the project leader of the hunger and homeless campaign for NYPIRG, and giving back has always been important to me. I cannot thank the EOP program at Buffalo State enough because I am part of a greater mission with my career to help encourage other women strive for success in the STEM field.

Sincerely,
Tanjin Minar

Senior Quality Engineer
Raytheon Technologies
Buffalo state Alumni 2018

Dear Mr. Eve,

My name is Anany Marcano, and I am both a student athlete as well as an EOP scholar here at Buffalo State. I am a freshman and had the pleasure of participating in the EOP summer program this year right before the semester began. The EOP program so far has been exceptional in the way it's helped me navigate and manage through all the ups and downs that come with being a first year.

I am forever grateful for being able to attend in the summer program and to have gotten a taste of what was to come. It set me up with a foundation that I've successfully been able to build on as the semester progresses. Having an active counselor has helped tremendously with my bills, registering for classes, and merely overall guidance. From both the summer and first semester of school, EOP has taught me numerous techniques and tips that I've used and can definitely vouch for. As well as allowing me to uncover myself some specific habits that I've found work best. The EOP ACE program as well has helped me numerous times. At first I thought it would be a hassle to have to go but I genuinely can focus there and have received wonderful help with my work that has excelled me as well.

EOP has helped not only financially but both academically and socially for me as well, and I'm so grateful for being able to receive these blessings at Buffalo State.

Sincerely,
Anany

MEMORANDUM FOR RECORD

FROM: 2d Lt Shamiqua Mason 914 FSS/FSF
SUBJECT: Letter of Appreciation/ My EOP Journey

I became a part of EOP family my freshmen year, Fall of 2001. At that time I had no clue how much of a blessing that was. I enlisted in the Air Force earlier that year, but my mom changed her mind about letting me go (I was only 17). She made me promise her I would try college. So I found myself at Buffalo State College hating every second of it.

I was honestly just going through the motions. My grades began to reflect that. I found myself on academic probation on more than one occasion. My EOP counselors were encouraging and tried to help motivate me, but I simply did not appreciate what I had nor did I want to be there. In 2004, I learned I was expecting and just stopped showing up to school. I gave up.

In 2007 I decided that I wanted to give school a real shot if not for myself for my daughter. I wanted to give her a better life. However, due to the way I left school, I accrued a debt that was difficult to pay as a single parent mom. Going back to school was not as easy as I thought, my poor grades were also a problem. So I began saving money and I decided to follow my heart and enlisted in the Air Force in March 2011.

When I came home, I worked hard to get back into school. I spent many days in meetings with admissions, academic standings, and other departments. My last stop was the EOP office. I was nervous it would take forever to get back in the program. I knew I needed support to reach my goal and felt ashamed that I had it but didn't appreciate it. I'm pretty sure I cried when Mr. William Ortega said to me, "Once EOP, always EOP." I finally returned to school Spring of 2013.

I received my Bachelor's degree in May 2014, a decade

after giving up and leaving school. I graduated with honors. I will never forget the look on my daughter's face, she was so proud of me. The EOP office helped me every step up of the way and encouraged me to consider graduate school. I applied for the Graduate Opportunity Program and graduated with my Masters in May 2019.

There are not enough words to express the gratitude I have for the EOP program. In September 2019, I went from enlisted to officer in the United States Air Force through the Deserving Airmen Program. This could not be possible without a degree. My counselors believed in me when I did not believe in myself. I went from zero degrees to three degrees. EOP helped me get two of them. I promote the EOP program wherever I go. I have referred my students, my troops, and honestly anyone I meet interested in college to the program.

Many people helped me achieve the life I live today, but the EOP program will always have a special place in my heart. Thank you Mr. Eve for creating a program that helped a little girl from the projects of Buffalo's lower west side become a leader and mentor with a genuine passion for helping others just like you helped me.

SHAMIQUA D. MASON, 2d Lt, USAF
Wing Yellow Ribbon Coordinator

To Arthur O. Eve,

I'm so happy to have the opportunity to thank you Mr. Eve.
Coming from a low income family with no opportunities to go
to college, the EOP program was a life changer for our family.
My oldest sister was in the program and went on to receive 2
Ph.D.'s, one in Library Science where she took a position as a
Federal Court librarian and another Ph.D. in Law, where she
worked as an attorney for a distinguished Buffalo law firm. My
sister Rita was also an EOP recipient, and she also has a Ph.D.
in Higher Education and is an Assistant Dean. Then my sister
Mary took advantage of the program and the day care at
Buffalo State, and she too has a Ph.D. and is a successful life
coach and hospital administrator. These sisters encouraged me
at one of the lowest points in my life to go to college. I had 2
children under 4 and no income. I received my GED because I
quit high school in the beginning of my junior year. With my
sisters' encouragement about their great results from the EOP
program, I too went to Buffalo State and graduated in 1989
with a BS in Food Systems Management. The summer
program to help the freshman learn about college and academics was very helpful. I credit my EOP counselor Roz
Berkovitz and my major advisor Lori Till with my success at
school. They were inspiring and encouraging when I needed it
the most. After graduating, I worked at Canisius College as a
supervisor before getting another job at M&T bank where I
have been for 20 years. The EOP program paid for my books,
day care, transportation and helped with a student loan prepay-
ment. None of which I could have afforded myself. I think the
program gave me hope, confidence and strength as a single low
income mother. I hope I'm an encouragement to my children to
persevere as I did. I hope you know how much and how many

students and families you have helped thru the years and how our lives have changed for the better because of the EOP program.

Bless you and yours.

Thanks,
Robin Brown
M&T Securities, Inc.
Account Services | Securities Operations Senior Associate

Dear Honorable Arthur O. Eve, Sr. Former Deputy Speaker of the New York State Assembly,

I am so grateful to be able to write to you. Your diligence and legal work in the New York State Assembly laid the foundation that dramatically enhanced my life and career. The following is a small excerpt from my memoir that sets the scene on how it all started for me:

"I had an extremely active schedule academically, including afterschool programs, where I earned enough school credits to almost have two high school diplomas. My class placement was in the top 25 senior students. I served in church with the same fierce pace as my schooling. I was in a leadership position in the young missionary group, and I sang in various choirs.

So, at the end in June 1970 after my high school graduation, why was I not accepted into any of the 4 colleges I applied for???????"

I remembered sitting in my living room for several weeks staring at the Sunday newspaper contemplating on reading the employment pages. I commenced the plans of looking for a job because, college was not in my reach.

My older sister was attending Rosary Hill College, under the Higher Equal Opportunity Program (HEOP), that you initiated with the government grants for higher education. Rosary Hill is presently called, Daemen College. My grandmother called and asked for Sister Mary Frances Welch who coordinated all HEOP students. I met Sister Mary the year before while my older sister was touring Rosary Hill. She remembered me and saw that I could qualify to come to Rosary Hill. But, the 'Hill' had filled their quota and Sister Mary pleaded my case to the college to accept one more. This took many weeks to sort out and by then, I was getting a little depressed that I was not going to attend a college in the fall.

At the end of July, I got a call to come to do an interview and attend an HEOP orientation for in-coming freshmen. Sister Mary, from that point on, hovered over me using all the available resources that the HEOP had to help me. You see, my placement was funded by all the leftover grant money that was not used by the other HEOP students. I did have to take out a small loan of $1,200.00 that covered when there were no funds left.

I could tell she wanted me to succeed and that motivated me to work hard. A few years later, she explained to me that there were many college staff members rooting for HEOP to fail. I was eager to participate and attended all that was offered to me.

It was like whatever I needed or dreamed I needed, HEOP was there for me to assist me to succeed. My former principal from East High School, Dr. Robert J. Rentz, was my advisor. He knew me personally. He was familiar with the East side of Buffalo, NY community, and he supported the other students in the program as well. He helped me overcome a racially charged situation in one of my freshmen class courses. That was my most memorable moment.

I was taking a Children's Literature class. The professor ridiculed me in front of everyone because she did not believe anything good came from African American and other minorities' literature. My plan was to design a children's anthology based off of minority authors; people from the Black, Brown, Yellow, and Red races. She told me that if I tried to do this, that would be an automatic "F" for the whole course. I told Dr. Rentz about this incident in class, and he encouraged me to start my project and do my best work.

The Book Lover's Club and my grandmother helped me

collect over 400 names of authors representing my focus groups, and we divided on white construction paper 4 columns posting in red, black, and green ink their names, date of written work, and title. This was the background paper for my bulletin board I was required to do. Then, I picked pictures, male and females, 4 from each race, and placed them on top of the background paper.

As sure as the professor promised, she wrote in very large print a huge "F" on the score card next to my bulletin board. I reported this to my advisor. He reviewed my project and told me to hold on. I got the message to meet him at the bulletin board site at a certain time. The Book Lover's Club members and my grandmother came too. We all stood there and the President of Rosary Hill College walked up the hallway to evaluate my board. She studied it and let out several ahh's, stating that I was sharing information most people didn't know about. She asked me for a red marker. Then, she wrote over the "F" grade and entered an "A+". She told me to be prepared to do a presentation of the best project for this class on Monday.

The design of HEOP provided for the students a strong support system of tutoring in the academics, counseling, complete financial package for school supplies, fees, and tuition costs. It opened the door for me to come live on campus and find full and part time employment while I studied. Since my major was elementary education, I chose to work as a pre-k teacher for all the 4 years in college. I graduated from Rosary Hill College with honors. I received the Who's Who Among Students in American Universities and Colleges, 1974. The benefits that HEOP provided me were a major contributor towards this achievement.

Reflecting on my HEOP experience, I can list numerous on-going milestones that had a powerful impact on me. I use them in my daily life and career. They are:

· The Higher Equal Opportunity Program saw potential in me when society did not open its door for me to go to college.

· The Higher Equal Opportunity Program provided administrators, teachers, and counselors who believed in its principles to be a great accommodating community surrounding me.

· The Higher Equal Opportunity Program Coordinator, Sister Mary F. Welch, personally became my surrogate parent advising me on how to cope in a place that was very different from my home. I had stepped outside of my community and was alone in so many ways. The statement, "It takes a village to raise a child," is so engrained into this program. I grasped on to her assistance because I needed it so much.

These concepts influenced my career as a teacher and my personal life. I saw in all my students something great in each of them. I fed that spark each time as I worked with them. I always sought after the parents, family members, and friends to corral a supportive community for my students. And, my mothering instincts were on high alert for not just my students but their parents too, making them feel my class was there to help them.

I earned a Master's degree and was accepted to do a Doctorate at SUNY @Buffalo. I taught for 45 years teaching all grades from pre-k to the college level. Several times, I received awards for my teaching excellence from the New York State Education Department, Buffalo Public School Board, educational magazines, and for my poetry.

I am now retired and an author of a faith- based children's book series called, <u>Puddinhead</u>. The children in the schools where I taught told me regularly after reading my books that they felt my stories showed them a time and place they would have loved to live in. The stories are passing on the messages behind the principles imbedded in the HEOP that in turn are inside me. I have a high regard for your faith walk within your public work.

Mr. Eve, you wrote your testimony in my 4th book, <u>Puddinhead's Daddy.</u> The confirming statements you made about how you were raised and who mentored you growing up in a single parent home have direct correlation to how the HEOP was designed. I thank you for passing on these wisdom practices through a state funded program and making life changing effects for so many people. You called me your angel but you were my angel first. God blessed you and used you and He is still looking after you.

A Heart Full of Gratitude,
Marilyn Foote-Kragbé

Dear Arthur O. Eve,

As a graduate of the Educational Opportunity Program (EOP) during the year of 1984, I would like to reflect and share my experiences as a student at Buffalo State. EOP helped me navigate and transition into my college life by providing counselors that assisted me with my financial aid package, as well as providing academic support with tutors. The Educational Opportunity Program also provided a community atmosphere for African-American students like me; similar to an environment you would find at Historically Black Colleges and Universities (HBCU).

The moment I remember most about the Educational Opportunity Program was during an EOP award ceremony. I had the pleasure of meeting Shirley Chisholm, who became the first black woman elected to the United States Congress and the first woman to run for the Democratic Party's presidential nomination. That moment gave me a sense of pride being an EOP student, and I also realized how important the honors recognition ceremony meant as an undergraduate.

What I learned through EOP as part of my everyday life is that no matter where you come from or the limited educational opportunities you may possess, as an EOP student you can be successful in the educational and corporate environments while leading a productive life in the community where you reside.

The lessons from the Educational Opportunity Program that I have passed on to the younger generation since graduation, is that EOP gave me a strong educational foundation to withstand challenges and adversity a person may experience in life while pursuing career and educational goals. Although I came from both an economic and educational disadvantage background as a student from Buffalo, New York, the Educational Opportunity Program instilled confidence and determination which motivated young African-American students to be successful in obtaining a college degree from Buffalo State as an EOP student.

Sincerely,

Arthur Scissum, '84
Rochester, NY

Dear Arthur O. Eve,

EOP for me provided the bridge that enabled me to transition to a successful graduate up to the master's level. It was only achievable because of the solid foundation and structured approach of the Summer program. My life changed for good when I walked through the hallowed halls of EOP in the Summer of 2004. My confidence as a freshman increased and so great was the value of the program that I was moved to serve as a peer advisor during my sophomore Summer so I could be a motivator for students coming in, whom I felt were having a similar perception to attending college early as I did. Certainly, making the transition from home and parental supervision to independence in a microcosm of the real world brings many challenges. In this higher level of academia, it's all self and time-management because no one is going to care more about your progress than you the individual. EOP provided the perfect conduit for creating a balance between study, rest and socializing. The program pushed me outside of my comfort zone and forced me to a well-disciplined approach to university life, and this pivotal start indeed played a significant role in my success as a student. My peers and I received the tools we needed to chart a successful and exciting course. The EOP ensured us access to everything we needed when we needed it.

My most memorable EOP memory was not having a phone or TV for the 6-week summer program. I instantly thought, "this is jail" lol. Those restrictions, however, were paramount to my success in college. When exams, papers and finals needed to be done, the common things that would be a distraction for most was easily dismissed for me and I was able to pour my energy into what needed to be done at the time! Something as simple as turning off my phone for 4 hours a day to disconnect and study made a huge difference in my academic performance and it showed across the board because EOP students performed above average in the college curriculum compared to our counterparts. There were many late-night library study sessions where I remembered seeing all my EOP family gearing up for finals, reminiscent of how we buckled down during our EOP summer program to ace our finals.

My EOP experience would be the strong and solid foundation I needed that propelled me to excel throughout my entire college career and beyond! EOP did not only prepare me to excel at the college level but in life! The core elements of responsibility, accountability, prioritizing, utilizing time management, self-care and cultivating meaningful healthy relationships was all developed and strengthened in my EOP 6-week summer program. I feel forever indebted to EOP for my achievement and successes throughout my whole career and outside of academics/ the professional world I developed relationships with people who are still near and dear to my heart till this very day!

Since graduation my eye lights up whenever I come across a young adult entering college and blessed with the opportunity of being a part of the EOP program. I always tell them, my EOP experience changed my life in such a positive way and it would definitely change theirs if they embrace the experience. I always acknowledge all the same fears and concerns I had when entering my summer program and let them know a major part of my successes as an adult was from the things I learned and the people I met in EOP! I embrace them and welcome them to the family!

Sincerely,
Kelly-Ann Redley
Stony Brook University

Dear Arthur O. Eve,

I came to America at the age of 6 with my mother, father, and younger sister from the Dominican Republic. Little did I know that life in the land of opportunities was going to be so difficult. I grew up seeing my mother and father struggle because they did not speak any English, and I knew I had to do something to help them. I dedicated my life to education and learning all I could to help my family. Time went on and I learned English and did well in high school, which led me to apply for college as a first-generation student. I was fortunate to get accepted into the Educational Opportunity Program which has opened many doors and provided me with the resources I need to succeed.

I thank you, Arthur. O Eve because your ambition to create an opportunity program for underprepared students has saved me. I would have never been able to succeed without the support that I received and continue to receive from the EOP family. Many people in this country want to do better, but unfortunately, their living consequences get in the way of their success. Having EOP helped me in many ways and I cherish every moment and all the people that I have met along the way. I was even able to get into Graduate School and get my tuition covered. I will forever be thankful for all the opportunities that I have had. I especially thank you, Mr. Eve, for your dedication and for creating such a special program for students like me to succeed.

Thank you form the bottom of my heart,

Sincerely,
Erika Mitchell

Assemblyman Eve,

Asante Sana, Muchas gracias, Merci mille fois, Molte grazie, Danke sehr, Dankuwel, Muito obrigado, Cok tesekkurler, Bol'shoye spasiba, Gan xie, jeong-mal go-ma-wo, Camon ban rat nhieu, Dah karam menna, Stokrotne dzieki, Doumo Arigatou gozaimasu, Iels paldies, Multumesc, Khawp jai, Salamat sa-LAH-mat, You are my hero, Dakujem mnohokrat, Puno hvala, Tak skal du have, You are so dope, Diky moc, Tanan vaga, kiitos paljon, Sas efharistovme, Mahalo nui loa, Shu-kri-yaa, Anda sungguh baik hati, Katta rahmat, Grazzi, Diolch yn fawr, Baie dankie, You are a life saver, Mesi, Tusen takk,Toda raba, Koszonom, Tena koe, Danko, Fa'afetai, Adupe, Na gode, Daalu nke ukwuu, Merci beaucoup, Grazie mille, Dankeschon, Dankjewel, Xie xie,Tesekkur ederim duo xie, Cam on, Hvala, You are everything, Thank you!

56 flavors of gratitude for 56 years of opportunity
Yanick Heriveaux Jenkins, Brockport State '86 and '87

Dear Arthur O. Eve,

I am writing to express my genuine gratitude and sincere thanks for creating the Educational Opportunity Programs, which sponsored my studies and provided me with mentorship to reach my full potential.

Because of the access and support, I have obtained my Doctorate Degree in Education and look forward to impacting lives. I am committed to continuing and mentoring it forward in your name.

Thank you again for all your thoughtfulness and for ensuring that education is seen from an equitable lens and that historically underrepresented and economically disadvantaged students are supported.

Sincerely,

Dr. Jean Leandre
Alumni, Educational Opportunity Center
Dean of Career and Professional Development

Dear Mr. Arthur O. Eve,

Thank you! Thank you! Thank you again! I would have not had the opportunity to retire after 36 years as an Educator of doing what I love if it had not been for EOP/HEOP. It allowed me to share with students and adults that you can be whatever you want to be despite your circumstances.

My doors opened through the EOP program. After going back to secure me GED and finishing at the top of the class, there was a community person sharing that if I had the chance would I be willing to go to College under a Program. This was always my dream to go to College, but circumstances always got in the way. I knew with this opportunity that I could not "blow it." My most memorial moment was when I matriculated out of a Social Studies class with the highest grade. This meant that I could go on to pursue my education in four (4) years and not five (5).

Not wanting to disappoint myself or the program, I attended every on- campus interview in November even though I was not scheduled to graduate until May with a BS in Special Education/ Elementary Education. My first positions were in Cleveland, Ohio, then to Atlanta, Georgia teaching in High School in the English Department, Youth Apprenticeship Facilitator, Support Teacher Specialist and Supervisor of Graduate students as they did their Internship. Doing what I loved allowed me to share with others. If it had not been for this Program, I would not have had the opportunity to share with young people what I had been through and given a chance you can become whatever you want to be. Just look at me- the first college graduate in my family from a mother who was a Domestic worker, a father who was a Mechanic and me, a divorced mom, raising four (4) daughters and receiving social assistance. This program gave me a chance of a lifetime to fulfill a dream I always had. It allowed me to let others know you can be whatever you want to be – given the opportunity. The EOP/HEOP did just that – "An Opportunity of a Lifetime".

Warm regards,
Carolyne J. Parks

Dear Arthur O. Eve,

You don't know me. I am a first generation American with parents from Dominica and Haiti. I was born and raised in Brooklyn, NY and figured out from a young age that I wanted to change the world. The problem, I didn't know how. There was no guidance, no cheat sheet, no info graphic, just instincts. As any first generation American and college student would say, we only knew about a handful of careers; doctor, lawyer, engineer. I thought, lawyer would be great, until I took a course called "Sociology of Law" and well my path was derailed. It took another year for me to find where I would affect social change. I doubled down, focusing solely on higher education, exploring access, opportunity, and success. For over five years, I worked in higher education, guiding students across the stage. I blazed across the institutions that employed me, often dubbed the fire starter. Then, I found EOP, I found you. A fire starter who created space, opportunity, and access for students. Students I dedicated my career to support. With EOP, I found a place where my fire wouldn't be snuffed out.

My path to you was unconventional. While most admire you as a recipient of the program you carried on your back, I found you in my journey toward fulfilling the promise I made to myself back in my undergraduate years. I found my métier, here in EOP. A space that you designed to be so broad with a laser focus to ensure students, educators, and researchers alike had somewhere blaze and grow. Somewhere to make a change.

Thank you for your work and for paving the way for me and many other scholars who fight daily to carve out space in the system of higher education to ensure all students have access and opportunity to succeed. As EOP has made so much room for my professional success, I often think, you do know me. You knew the struggle and you did something about it.

In Solidarity,

Abigail Bryant

Dr. Eve,

I cannot say thank you enough for a program like EOP! I have always said once you're EOP, you're always EOP.

As an Alumna of Buffalo State, I would not have made it a second time if it was not for the DYNAMIC team in the program. This team has watched me fail only to succeed again! They have guided me in the correct steps I needed to go in to be a successful student. Once I graduated, they became family! Everyone was at my wedding, they have embraced my Twin Granddaughters, been there for me in every accomplishment in my life! So it's not just the benefits of the program you are getting...IT'S AN ENTIRE FAMILY that you have!!!! I LOVE MY EOP, not only what they have done for me. It's what they continue to do for those students that are like me!!!

Sincerely,

Taiya Mouzon
Buffalo State Alumni
Class of 2007

Mr. Arthur O. Eve,

My name is Lana James, and I am a Buffalo State University EOP (Educational Opportunity Program) Alumni student. I graduated from the institution in 2011 with an undergraduate degree in Sociology and a master's in human service administration. The EOP Program has been the foundation of my educational journey and success. The program housed the supportive staff that I needed in unfamiliar territory as a first-year student in college. These same staff would later become more like family.

As a sophomore in college, I began working for a pre-collegiate support program STEP (Science Technology Entry Program) tutoring high school students. During this time, I also attended tutoring sessions in the EOP Department. I was able to share the support and guidance given to me with others (high school students). I later moved into the secretarial position and then the program coordinator position for the STEP Program, holding a 15-year tenure.

My relationship with the EOP Program continued during my time. We are now able to work closely with the department, ensuring that high school students are exposed and be the bridge for entry into the program.

My educational journey did not stop. In 2019 I gained a Licensed profession certificate and opened a Spa, holding a successful and flourishing beauty business.

Such programs hold an immense amount of value to a student's educational growth and success. It gave me the comfort, the reassurance, and the guidance I needed to navigate college and has been the framework for my career.

As an adult that same guidance has continued. Mrs. Jenkins, EOP Director, is now a model and a guide in my adulthood and for that I will always be grateful and continue to give the same support that has been given to me and to others.

A heartfelt Thank you Mr. Arthur O Eve and Happy Birthday. May you be blessed in your lifetime!

Lana James, EOP ALUMNA

Dear Dr. Arthur O. Eve,

I recall as one of the first EOP students to receive the invite to attend SUNY Brockport as a freshman, you graced us with your presence, along with Mr. Norman McConney, to encourage us to succeed in completing our college education. Twelve years later, you took the time to greet this new Director of a new HEOP Program, at Niagara University in Niagara Falls, New York. You often visited the college to assist me while I was at Niagara University, in building a viable HEOP Program. Then, in 1985, you along with my friends Norman McConney and Robert James welcomed me, back where I began, as the Director of the EOP Program at SUNY Brockport.

Words cannot express what you have done for persons like myself and the inspiration, help, encouragement, and wisdom, you provided me and so many others. I am grateful and I give thanks to God for your leadership, your courage and your friendship through these years.

Thank you and may you be continually blessed.

Sincerely,

Gary Owens
Director of EOP
SUNY Brockport

Dear Arthur O. Eve,

I come to you with sincere gratitude and thanks as an EOP Alum class of 02' and 04 from Buffalo State where you had the honor and privileges of starting the program. As a young Black girl that grew up in New York City Housing in Brooklyn, NY attending college was always my dream. When I learned that I was admitted into Buffalo State's program I was elated. This would be the start of my new journey toward achieving my goal of obtaining professional greatness.

During my time at Buffalo State, I had the honor and privilege of working for EOP under the leadership of Mrs. Yanick Jenkins and Mrs. Maria Brickhouse. Both Mrs. Jenkins and Mrs. Brickhouse embodied all that EOP strives for which is helping young people reach their fullest potential. As an EOP student, I was able to be my authentic self by not only giving back to the program that helped me through my ability to serve as their Spanish tutor and front desk receptionist but later on as the Resident Director for the EOP summer program. These experiences coupled with my friendship with your granddaughter, Shiana, helped to increase my love for all that you have done to ensure that alum like me had the opportunity to obtain a quality education.

As an EOP graduate, I have gone on to obtain my doctorate. I now work in higher education by choice. This career change came once I decided that I wanted to be the conduit to help others be successful. It is my goal to give back and support as many students as possible by sharing my love, guidance, and the education I gained while working for and being an EOP student. The program that you have created is necessary, especially in today's society. It is necessary as it can be hard for underserved students to know their worth, especially in a world filled with filters and reality tv that don't show the real reality of life. Whenever possible I always share my experience with EOP and how grateful I am to you and your vision for what EOP could be. It is because of you that I now serve on various committees to help shape the policies and procedures for many institutions to help ensure that all students get a quality education. For that, I say thank you Mr. Arthur O. Eve for your vision and all that you do, Happy 90th Birthday.

Warmest Regards,

Dr. LaToya Blount
EOP Alum
Buffalo State 02', 04'

Dear Mr. Eve,

I want to express my gratitude to EOP. Without EOP, I would not have been able to attend college. As an immigrant student, a college is only sometimes an option because it is too expensive. Especially when there are multiple children in a household. With EOP, college was an option for me because it helped with tuition, textbooks, and other educational needs. I am forever grateful for EOP. Even today, whenever I hear someone mention EOP, I get excited and always follow up with, "I was an EOP student too." It was a privilege and honor to be an EOP student. I am forever grateful.

Warm Regards,

Javon Joslyn
Interim Director of Haverstraw Center

Dear Mr. Eve,

I have so much gratitude for you and the Educational Opportunity Program you started. I am beyond thankful and know that without EOP, I would not be the woman I am today.

As a product of a single parent household, my mother worked two jobs to support my sisters and myself. With only a high school education, she knew very little about college. By the time I was ready to start exploring colleges, my sister was already an EOP student at Buffalo State. I don't believe my mother knew exactly what EOP was or how they were helping my sister, but she knew it was a good thing. So much so that when I visited the college I would attend, my mother was insistent that we talk to someone in EOP and that I be considered for the program. Knowing my sister qualified, she knew I would, too.

Two months into my freshman year, I lost my mother. I was a freshman at Genesee Community College at the time, and there was someone who oversaw the EOP program but I didn't have an assigned counselor. Two years later, I transferred to Brockport State where I would meet my EOP Counselor, Wilma Boddie-Beaman. In my first meeting with Wilma, she told me that she would now be like a second mother to me. She wasn't lying... I spent the next three years struggling academically as I also struggled to process the grief of losing my mother, the home I knew, and my family with my sisters. I felt so alone trying to navigate my new world, but Wilma became my one constant. She provided me with the love I was missing in my life. I tell people that EOP saved my life and specifically Wilma saved my life. She provided me with loving support I needed to succeed. She helped to pull me out of one of the darkest periods of my life. She provided me with unconditional love, tough love when I needed it and countless lunches and dinners when she thought I wasn't taking care of myself. Most of all, Wilma provided me with the patience I needed to find my way in the world.

After barely making it out of undergrad, six years later, I returned to Wilma for advice on Graduate School. She worked with me and coached me for the rigorous interview that was required by the Counselor Education Department at Brockport. With Wilma's support and encouragement once again in my life, I was admitted into the program and graduated with my Master's. This would not have been possible if it wasn't for the GOP waiver that was offered to EOP students applying for graduate work.

Twenty-nine years later, I sit in Wilma's chair as a Senior EOP Counselor, and I know she is looking down on me smiling. I am just one of many students whose life was transformed from being part of this EOP family. I am forever grateful to you, Mr. Eve, not only for creating EOP but for your continued efforts throughout your life to advocate for this amazing program.

Sincerely,
Carole Miller-Canestrari

A POEM FOR MR. EVE

A GIANT STEP
By Cynthia Mathews

(Dedicated to Assemblyman Arthur O' Eve, who
may have lost the battle, but surely won the war
during his 1977 campaign for Mayor, and who
successfully awakened the Black Community to a
state of unified consciousness.)

A Giant stepped
Amongst us,
He waved his
Mighty hand,
He gathered all
The people
To give them
His great plan.

They could not
Understand him
For his wisdom
Was far-fetched,
But
They listened attentively
To every word
He said.

Now education,
Unemployment, and
Housing
Were clearly on his mind,
But
He understood the
People had problems
And their hopes had
Begun to decline.

The people
Looked bewildered.
How puzzled
They were left!
For, how could
This man from
All the rest
Guarantee them the best?

"I'll tell you,"
He answered,
With his hands
Stretched out to God.
"I'm sincere in
My plan,
But
I'll need your
Help as well."

"What can we do?"
Most proclaimed.
While others
Only laughed.

"You can give me
Your VOTE,
On September Eighth,
My dear brother man."

"Who are you?"
Shrieked this little
Voice from behind
The pack.

"Why I'm the EVE
Of awakening."
He quietly
Answered back.

"He looks OK,"
Some whispered;
Some just gazed
And glanced.

"I don't know."
Said this little old man,
"There's something
About his color
That I'm still not
Sure of, yet."

"Why I'm just
A Black giant,"
The man humbly said,
"No different
From any other,
Whether he be
White, Yellow, or Red."

"I'll help you,"
Said one man,
As he PUSH-ed
Through the crowd.
"Far I believed
We will achieve,"
He shouted very loud.

"Take this giant step
With me," he pleaded
One more time.
"We will overcome
The hazards
Which overcome
Your mind."

The people began
To welcome,
The dawn of
This new way –
They held their
Hands in unity
And
Awaited that final day.

September 8, 1977

BIBLIOGRAPHY

*** All books, photographs, and articles obtained during the course of my research have been donated to SUNY Buffalo State's Butler Library.

Boyd, Herb. Gore Singles Out Deputy Speaker for Praise. *New York Amsterdam News*, New York, N.Y. April 23 5:1. (1998)

Borrelli, George et al. Democrats Interview 2 Mayoral Candidates. *Buffalo News*, Buffalo, N.Y. January 21. (1989)

Campagna, Darryl. City to Get New Schools. *Buffalo News [Final Edition]*, Buffalo, N.Y. December 28, A1. (2000)

Carton, P. A Black Man Runs for Mayor: The Extraordinary Campaign of Arthur O. Eve. Afro-Americans in New York Life and History (1977-1989), 4(2), 7. Retrieved from: http://proxy.buffalostate.edu:2048/login?url=https://search.proquest.com/docview/219949794?accountid=7259. (1980)

Cichon, Steve. Buffalo in the '60s: Buffalo's leaders urge peace following King's Assassination. *Buffalo News*, March 14. (2016)

Cornell. Arthur O. Eve Opportunity Programs. https://oadi.cornell.edu/programs/student-opportunity-programs/arthur-o-eve-opportunity-programs/about-eop-heop/who-is-arthur-oeve.html. (2019)

Eve, Arthur O. A Message of No Hope. *New York Amsterdam News*, New York, N.Y. 11 March 1995, p. 12. (1995)

Farley, Ena L. The African American Presence in the History of Western New York. In *Afro-Americans in New York Life and History*, Volume 14, (1):27. (1990)

Farrell, William E. 2 Years of Racial Protest Stall Buffalo Campus Project, Special to *The New York Times*, September 18, p. 45. (1970)

Gates, George and Phil Fairbanks. Amos, Bell Claim Attempts to Discredit Them. *Buffalo News*, Buffalo, N.Y. January 27. (1989)

Hicks, Jonathan P. Longtime Assemblyman Announces He Will Not Seek Re-Election. *The New York Times*, March 25, B4. (2002)

Institute for Latino Studies. September 9, 2016. Arthur O. Eve, First Dominican Elected to Public Office in USA, To Be Honored with The Illustrious Lifetime Achievement Award for Service in Politics. http://instituteforlatinostudies.org/2016/09/first-dominican-elected-to-public-office-in-usa-has-been-nominated-for-the-illustrious-lifetime-achievement-award-for-service-in-politics-2/. (2016)

Jeffries JL. The New York State Black and Puerto Rican Legislative Caucus,

1970-1988. Afro-Americans in New York Life and History, Volume 24(1):7. (2000)

Kraus, Jeffrey. Eve, Arthur Owen. The Encyclopedia of New York State, p. 536, edited by Peter Eisenstadt and Laura-Eve Moss. Syracuse University Press. (2005)

Levy, Elizabeth and Mara Miller. POLITICIANS FOR THE PEOPLE: Six Who Stand for Change. Dell Publishing Company, Inc. (1981)

Long Island Business News. NY Assembly considers tax amnesty legislation. (Government) *Long Island Business News,* May, Volume 49, Issue 21. (2002)

Mallegg, Kristin B. (Editor). Eve, Arthur O. Who's Who Among African Americans, 23rd Edition, p. 383. Gale Cengage Learning. (2009)

Montgomery, David. Essentially Eve. *The Buffalo News.* November 14. (1992)

Neuman, William. Dominican Candidates for Congress Claim Pioneer Status, but History Is Complex. *New York Times,* June 28, A20(L). (2016)

NY Senate. NY State Senate resolution honoring Arthur O. Eve on his being designated as a recipient of a Liberty Medal. https://legislation.nysenate.gov/pdf/bills/2017/J4741. (2018)

NY State Special Commission (NYSSC). Attica: The Official Report of the New York State Special Commission on Attica. Bantam Books, New York. (1972)

O'Donnell, Neil. Helping Students Prepare for Fall Semester Success. *The Facilitating Tutor* Vol. 1(1), p. 1. (2012)

Precious, Tom. State Funding Teacher Pay $45 Million Bailout Ends Long Struggle Over Lawsuit. *The Buffalo News, City Edition.* June 9. (2000)

Precious, Tom. With Passion, Less Clout, Eve Pushes for Tutoring. *The Buffalo News, Final Edition.* September 7, B1. (2003)

Schulman, Susan. Despite earlier reports, Eve reaffirms support for hallway house for inmates. *The Buffalo News, City Edition.* May 28. (1993)

Siener, William H. Buffalo. In *The Encyclopedia of New York State,* p. 233, edited by Peter Eisenstadt and Laura-Eve Moss. Syracuse University Press. (2005)

Taylor, Steven J.L. Desegregation in Boston and Buffalo. SUNY series in Afro-American studies. (1998).

The future of Black Studies: comments in celebration of Black History Month. Vital Speeches of the Day. 59.17, June 15, p. 536. (1993)

Thompson, Heather Ann. *Blood in the Water: The Attica Uprising of 1971 and Its Legacy.* Vintage Books, New York. (2016)

Thompson, Carolyn (Associated Press). Assembly veteran Eve to retire after 35 years: [THREE STAR Edition]. *The Times Union,* Albany, N.Y., Mar 24, D5. (2002)

Watson, Rod. Getting Kids to Read is Up to The Parents. *The Buffalo News,* January 12. (2005)

Weiss, Samuel. Education Watch; a Report Card for Cuomo's First Term. *New York Times*, 1986.

Wicker, Tom. A Time to Die: The Attica Prison Revolt (reprint from 1975 and 1994 editions). Haymaker Books, Chicago, Illinois. (2011)

Williams, Lillian S., Amybeth Gregory and Hadley Kruczek-Aaron. African Americans. The Encyclopedia of New York State, pp. 18-25, edited by Peter Eisenstadt and Laura-Eve Moss. Syracuse University Press. (2005)

Given an Opportunity
ISBN: 978-4-82418-766-6

Published by
Next Chapter
2-5-6 SANNO
SANNO BRIDGE
143-0023 Ota-Ku, Tokyo
+818035793528

29th September 2023

Printed in the USA
CPSIA information can be obtained
at www.ICGtesting.com
LVHW041945031123
762909LV00004B/32